Freshwater Fish & Fishing

by Jim Arnosky

Illustrated by the Author

FOUR WINDS PRESS
NEW YORK

A special thanks to Barbara

To Deanna, Michelle, and Amber,
for listening to all my fish stories

LIBRARY OF CONGRESS CATALOGING IN PUBLICATION DATA

Arnosky, Jim.
Freshwater fish & fishing

Summary: Describes different varieties of freshwater fishes
and instructs how to catch them.
1. Fishing—Juvenile literature. 2. Fishes, Freshwater—Juvenile literature. [1. Fishes, Freshwater. 2. Fishing] I. Title. II.
Title: Freshwater fish and fishing.
        SH445.A76   799.1'1   81-12520
        ISBN 0-590-07799-6   AACR2

PUBLISHED BY FOUR WINDS PRESS

A DIVISION OF SCHOLASTIC INC., NEW YORK, N.Y.

COPYRIGHT © 1982 BY JAMES ARNOSKY

PRINTED IN THE UNITED STATES OF AMERICA

LIBRARY OF CONGRESS CATALOG CARD NUMBER: 81-12520

1   2   3   4   5   86   85   84   83   82

Contents

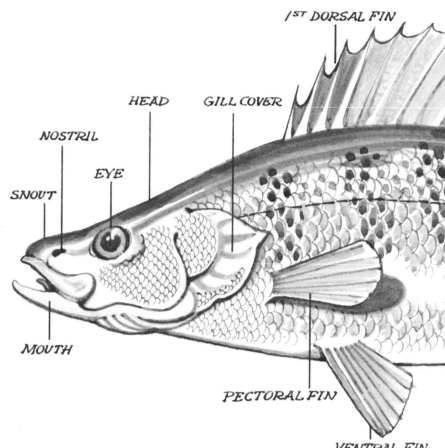

NOSTRIL

SNOUT

EYE

HEAD

GILL COVER

1ST DORSAL FIN

MOUTH

PECTORAL FIN

VENTRAL FIN

Parts of a Typical Fish

Fish smell with their nostrils. They breathe by gulping water into their mouths and filtering air from it with their gills. If you have an aquarium, you can watch the fish opening and closing their gill covers as they breathe.

4

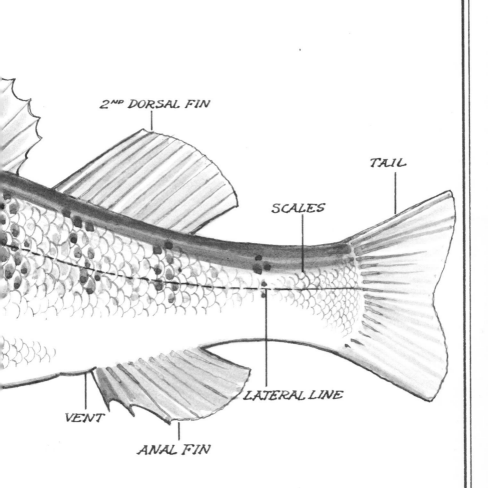

2ᴺᴰ DORSAL FIN

TAIL

SCALES

LATERAL LINE

VENT

ANAL FIN

A fish swims by wiggling its tail and body in sideways motion. Those with streamlined bodies are the fastest swimmers. The large fin on a fish's back is the dorsal fin. The fin on its bottom, near the tail, is the anal fin. These act as a keel and keep the fish upright in the water. The pectoral fins on a fish's sides help it swim up or down. The ventral fins below them are used for stopping and for balance while turning.

Introduction

There are freshwater fish and saltwater fish. The difference between them is a chemical one. Salt is an important body chemical. Too little salt or too much salt is unhealthy.

Salt is scarce in freshwater. A freshwater fish's system works to retain the level of body salt needed for a healthy balance.

A saltwater fish is bombarded by salt. Its system works to expel any amount of salt absorbed that is above the level needed to stay healthy.

Some fish, like salmon and shad, can live in both fresh and salt waters. They are able to adapt their body systems to the amount of salt in the water around them. These fish are called "anadromous" fish.

This book is about fresh water and some freshwater fish. The fresh waters include the clear,

cold waters that trout prefer; the quiet, weedy ponds where sunfish live; and the muddy creek bottoms where catfish lie.

When I'm fishing I always reel in more nature than fish. I've watched a watersnake slowly swallow a fat sunfish on a Pennsylvania stream bank. I've tiptoed past a bear cub napping on a sunny lakeshore in Vermont and felt a school of tiny bream nibble at my bare toes in a Florida pond.

I've shared my secret fishing spots with splashing beavers and drinking deer. Now I want to share it all with you—the fish, the fishing, and the wonders of the freshwater world.

Jim Arnosky

RAMTAILS, 1982

Trout

The high country lake is still as glass and shrouded in mist. It is fed by springs deep within the nearby mountains. Suddenly a dimple forms on the water. Soon the lake is perking with rising fish. The mist lifts and a fish leaps. Its speckled side flashes in the first glow of morning. A deer appears on the shore. Her heart-shaped hooves imprint the bank as she sips the ice-cold water. The lake's sandy bottom flickers in penetrating sunlight. This is trout water.

Of all the finny tribes, trout are the purists. They dwell only in the coldest and clearest of our fresh waters. Look for them in high country ponds and deep lakes, in tumbling mountain brooks, and in spring-fed rivers. The three most common trout are the brook trout, rainbow trout, and brown trout. It is possible to find all three living together if the water is colder than 70°F and rich in underwater insect life, a necessary food for all trout.

Trout are magical and mystical. They are the fish of storybooks. One glance at the dappling of colors on their streamlined bodies and it is easy to believe in enchanted princes and hidden treasure.

KINGFISHER
WITH MINNOW

NEWT

BROWN TROUT

CRAYFISH

MAYFLY

RAINBOW TROUT

BROOK TROUT

CADDIS WORMS
IN THEIR CASES

BLACKNOSE DACE
MINNOWS

MAYFLY NYMPH

The **Brook Trout** was the only trout for the early settlers of New England and still is the native trout of our eastern waters. Adult "brookies" average from six to ten inches. They live in the coldest spring streams and woodland ponds. There, amid moss-black boulders and forest greens, they appear jewellike.

Brookies are eager eaters. Many times I've seen two or more break the surface at once, chasing insects in a kind of watery ballet. Mayflies, caddis flies, and the juvenile stages of both are brook-trout foods. The next time you are in a clear stream, turn over some stones and look for tiny mayfly nymphs clinging to the undersides.

MAYFLY
NYMPH

Mayflies are insects that live the first part of their lives underwater as nymphs. Nymphs crawl on the stream bottom for a year or more. Finally, when the temperature of the water and the time of the year are right, they swim to the surface. Their skins are shed and they float on the water's surface until their new wings dry. Then they fly off. Safe on shore they shed still another skin after which they mate, in air, with other mayflies. The males die. The females deposit their eggs on the water. Then the females also die. But the eggs sink to the stream bottom and eventually hatch as nymphs, starting the cycle over.

WINGED
MAYFLY

While hunting nymphs under rocks, you may also find some caddis worms inside the cases they make of tiny pebbles, leaf parts, or sticks. Hidden in their "mobile homes," the young larvae

CADDIS WORM

CADDIS WORMS
IN PEBBLE CASES

12

of caddis flies cling to stream boulders. Sometimes they lose hold and are carried downstream where hungry trout gobble them, case and all.

WINGED CADDIS FLY

Brook trout spawn in late fall when the females swim upstream to lay eggs among the pebbles of the streambed. After the eggs are fertilized by milt, a fluid from the male's body, they are abandoned. Baby fish are called fry. Newly hatched trout fry face many dangers. Those that avoid fishing birds, raccoons, and the jaws of larger trout, grow and become very wary. Because of this, trout fishing calls for a silent approach which often pays extra in chance meetings with other shy creatures along the water. You may see a dainty yellow-throated warbler flitting from branch to branch, or spot a brilliant red eft salamander crawling over a gnarled root.

RED EFT

The **Rainbow Trout** is native west of the Rocky Mountains but through transplanting has become our most popular trout. You probably have rainbows in the trout streams near you. Rainbow trout tolerate water slightly warmer than brook trout do, and they can thrive in open unshaded waters.

These acrobatic fish are named for the rainbow on each side of their bodies. It flashes pink, silver, and blue as they leap high out of water after airborne insects. Besides insects, rainbow trout eat minnows and crayfish. Adults range from eight to fourteen inches and, where they can

13

swim from smaller streams into big rivers and lakes, they may grow as long as two feet or more. The heavy and powerful steelhead fish are simply anadromous rainbow trout that have migrated to the sea and back.

Rainbows spawn in spring when the water is high. They like swift water in general. Pick a spot along a stream and watch the riffles. If rainbows are there, you'll notice their flipping tails and flashing sides. Watch closely and you may see what they are feeding on.

If you are stream-watching around sunset you may be startled by the splash of a big brown trout.

Brown Trout are the most elusive of all trouts. They favor slow-moving water and rarely feed before sundown. At night they gorge themselves on insects, minnows, crayfish, frogs, and even other trout. When a stream pool seems fishless, it may be that a huge brown has taken over— and other fish dare not enter.

The brown trout was brought to America from Europe in the 1800s. Once they are introduced in a stream, many will spawn each fall. Because of their large size and golden color, it is easy to spot a brown trout flashing through the water. If you notice such a flash, return at dusk to watch for surface activity.

I remember such a spot on my favorite stream. The evening was calm and the water smooth. I crawled on my elbows to the water's edge and watched for signs of a brown trout. A pale yellow mayfly sailed across the pool, like a tiny ship on a peaceful sea. Suddenly a brown trout appeared, suspended on an angle in the water just an inch below the mayfly ship. Together they drifted in the gentle current. As they neared my hiding place on the bank, the trout rose and sipped. A dimple formed. The ship was gone. For such a large fish it had barely made a swirl on the surface.

DRY FLY

FISHING FOR TROUT

Fish are finely tuned to their environment. They can feel the slightest movement in the water. Vibrations of any thumping sound made on the shore will spook them. Trout are the spookiest of all fish. Stay low so they won't see you. Keep your shadow off the water. Try not to make sudden movements. If you alarm them, they will stop feeding.

The best way to catch trout is to use a fly. This is a lure made of feathers or fur tied on a hook. "Dry" flies, tied light and bushy, float on the water like winged mayflies. "Wet" flies, tied with heavy wool yarn, sink and look like swimming nymphs. Long "streamer" flies imitate small minnows.

WET FLY

15

STREAMER

To try fly fishing you can use homemade flies or buy some at a store. Simply tie one on your line and crouch by the water. Lower the fly until it gently touches the surface and floats. A fish may rise and sip it down.

SPLIT-SHOT
SINKERS

Or you can let the fly get waterlogged and sink, and catch a fish as the fly drifts in the current. When the sunken fly reaches the end of its drift, make it swim back by pulling it, with short quick tugs. Remember to make it act like a natural insect and it will attract even the largest trout. If you want to cast a sinking fly, you can pinch a split-shot sinker on your line, about a foot above the fly. To cast a floating fly, attach a bobber three feet above your fly, to add the needed weight. Watch the fly as it floats on the water

SPLIT-SHOT   WET FLY

BOBBER   DRY FLY

near the bobber. When the fish sips at the fly, strike immediately. A fish will reject anything that feels unnatural in its mouth. If it feels the hook, it will spit it out.

NATURAL FLY

16

IMITATION FLY

You may want to try a fly rod and reel with a special floating fly line. With this equipment, the fly is tied to a six foot leader of transparent nylon line which is attached to the end tip of the floating fly line. The heavy fly line will have enough weight to cast the weightless nylon leader and tiny fly onto the water.

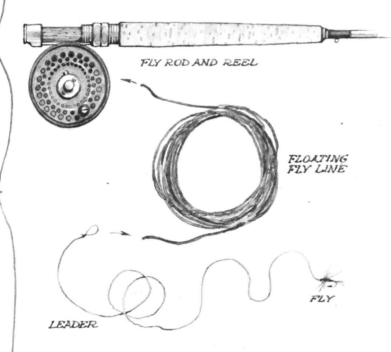

FLY ROD AND REEL

FLOATING
FLY LINE

LEADER

FLY

Wherever you fish, take time to learn the laws. Find out the legal size and number of fish that may be taken. The best part of fly fishing is that the fish you catch will be hooked only in the lip, so any you want to release can be set free.

17

TYING A FLY

Most fishing flies are tied starting with a tail, wrapping the body, adding wings, and finishing off with the head. To tie this simple fly you will need a small vise or locking pliers to hold the hook steady as you work.

Materials: Twenty inches of thread, a six-inch piece of yarn (I use yellow or brown), a feather from an old hat, a small hook, a pair of scissors, and waterproof glue.

Tie the thread onto your hook and knot it tight.

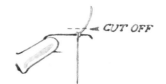

CUT OFF

Add a few wisps of feather for a tail and wrap them on with the thread. Knot it again.

Attach a tip of the yarn with another thread knot, then wrap both thread and yarn to the eye of the hook. Knot it firmly with the thread only.

Cut off the excess yarn and you have completed the body.

CUT OFF

Attach a small bunch of feather wisps on top of the yarn body for wings and wrap securely with thread.

Now finish off the fly's head with thread wraps. Knot it twice and cut off the remaining thread. To keep the knots secure, add a touch of glue to the fly's head and you are ready to try it out on some fish!

FINISHED FLY

Sunfish

When a trout stream leaves its forested birthplace and flows through open country, the water warms. Trout become scarce and schools of suckers horde the pools. Pickerelweed crowds mud-bottomed shores. The stream may feed a pond brimming with water lilies. Here mallards nest and spotted turtles shine on fallen logs. This is sunfish water.

Sunfish are oval shaped, heavily scaled, and have two dorsal fins that join together. These joined dorsal fins are a good way to recognize sunfish. The most common sunfish are bass, bluegills, pumpkinseeds, and crappies. Look for them in vegetated lakes and streams. They are at home in both farm pond and city reservoir.

Sunfish is a perfect name for this scrappy clan. Their weedy domain is warm with life. It is a world of swimming muskrats, bellowing frogs, and sunning snakes. Kick off your shoes, find a sunny spot, and read this chapter barefoot.

MALLARDS

DRAGONFLY

PUMPKINSEED

BLUEGILL

SMALLMOUTH BASS

DRAGONFLY NYMPH

PAINTED TURTLE

CRAPPIE

LARGEMOUTH BASS

SILVERY MINNOW

Pumpkinseeds are among the smallest sunfish. They average six inches long. Their bright yellow breast nicknames them "sunnies." You'll find them in quiet weedy ponds and sluggish streams.

Pumpkinseeds spawn during springtime, in very shallow water. This gives you a chance to watch them up close. All sunfish spawn the same way. The male clears a circular nest on the bottom of the pond. Here he coaxes a female to lay her eggs, which he fertilizes with milt. Then, alone, father fiercely guards his nest until the fry hatch and are big enough to be on their own.

When they are not spawning, pumpkinseeds live in small groups called schools. They feed at the bottom of the pond on insects and small snails. Sometimes pumpkinseeds swim up and feed on surface bugs the way their larger cousins do.

One of the pumpkinseed's larger cousins is a snappy little fish called a bluegill.

The **Bluegill,** or bream, has an orange breast and blue gills. Bluegills are slightly bigger than pumpkinseeds and live in vegetated lakes and ponds. Small schools of bluegills roam the water, eating many minnows, tadpoles, and bugs.

24

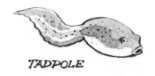

TADPOLE

Bluegills are curious. They will inspect any commotion in the water. If you sit on the bank and tap a long stick on the pond, nearby bluegills will come to it. This is how they find land bugs that have fallen onto the water. Struggling grasshoppers, bumblebees, and beetles are found and eaten by these curious fish. I have seen bluegills stick themselves right up out of the water to inspect a noise on a floating lily pad.

When a bluegill takes a bug off the surface, it makes a sharp snapping sound with its mouth. Listen for "snaps" in seedy shallow water and look for these sprightly little fish hovering there.

Bluegills spawn in springtime. You may find a bluegill nest when you are looking for pumpkinseeds.

Crappies are also sunfish that spawn in springtime shallows. But as soon as their spawning is over, they retreat to the deeper water they prefer. Larger schools of crappies live in deep holes of lakes and bayous. They are silvery fish, dappled with green and black.

Crappies grow to be twelve inches or longer. They like minnows best but will also catch and eat insects and crayfish. A crappie is not as easy to watch as a pumpkinseed or bluegill, because it hides in the nooks and crannies of submerged logs and tangled vegetation. All three of these sunfish will swim away, terrified, at the sight of the bully of the clan, the largemouth bass.

CRAYFISH

As soon as they are old enough to leave the nest, **Largemouth Bass** begin terrorizing the pond. They will gobble up anything that fits into their wide mouths. However, there is no reason for you to be afraid of them. They have no sharp teeth and will dash away if they see you. Largemouth bass like the same waters as bluegills. They live together in loose bands amid dead tree branches and under lily pads. Watch for V-shaped runs on the water. They could be formed by bass traveling close to the surface. Listen for loud *kerplunks* near the shore where bass hunt for frogs.

V-SHAPED RUN

Largemouths will keep growing as long as they live. Those that can escape fishing otters, ospreys, and people, live a long time. Most bass you see will be between ten and twenty inches. A largemouth bass can swallow anything from a dragonfly to a duckling.

One evening I was wading in a pond near my home. In the twilight I saw a mouse swimming. Suddenly the water swirled and the mouse disappeared in a watery *glunk*. A largemouth bass had gulped it down.

I have also seen largemouths swallow frogs, watersnakes, and even songbirds that had perched on branches too close to the pond. Bass stalk their prey like cats, advancing only inches at a time, until close enough to lunge.

Largemouth bass also spawn each spring in shallow water. They have a green back, white belly, and a black-dotted stripe along their sides. Their closest relative, the smallmouth bass, is slightly smaller, bronze-colored, and has no black stripe down its side.

LARGEMOUTH

SMALLMOUTH

Although **Smallmouth Bass** look and spawn like sunfish, they act more like trout. Smallmouths are more wary than their boisterous sunfish cousins. It takes a careful approach to watch them at home, in the clear, rocky parts of lakes and streams.

These bass eat more minnows than any other food, and rarely feed after dark the way largemouths do. Smallmouth bass are loners. Even as fry they seem fearless of other, larger fish. They cruise the shallows like finger-sized ruffians who know very well that, inch for inch, they are the strongest fish in the lake.

FISHING FOR SUNFISH

Because sunfish are curious, the best way to fish for them is to get their attention. There are many lures you can make or buy that will attract sunfish. Some flash or wiggle to look like minnows. Others swim in the water to look like snakes and mice. And there are lures that imitate surface bugs or plopping frogs.

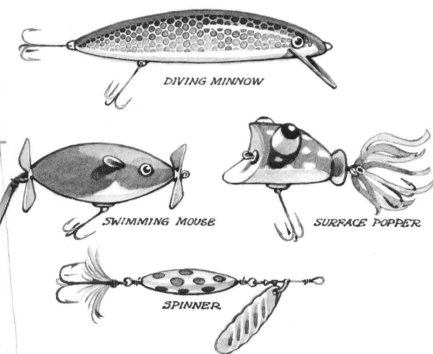

DIVING MINNOW

SWIMMING MOUSE

SURFACE POPPER

SPINNER

In bright daylight a lure called a spinner will catch fish. Spinners are metal lures that flash in the water. You can buy a spinner for less than fifty cents. They are the easiest lures to use. All you need is a rod, a reel, and the spinner.

SPINNING ROD
AND REEL

28

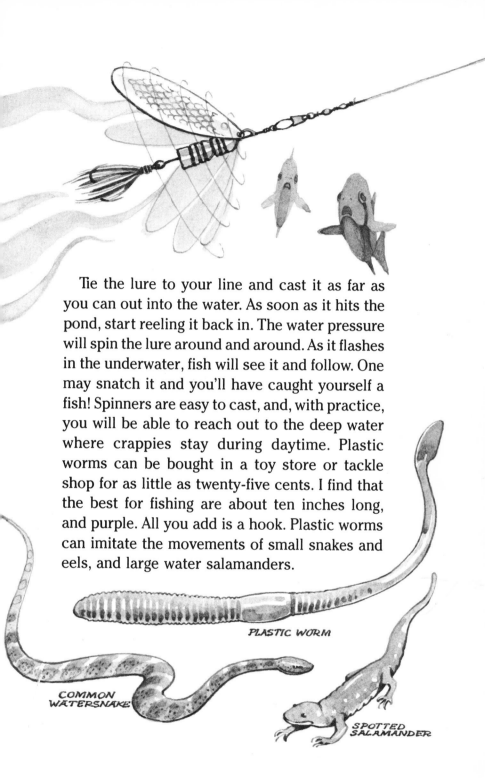

Tie the lure to your line and cast it as far as you can out into the water. As soon as it hits the pond, start reeling it back in. The water pressure will spin the lure around and around. As it flashes in the underwater, fish will see it and follow. One may snatch it and you'll have caught yourself a fish! Spinners are easy to cast, and, with practice, you will be able to reach out to the deep water where crappies stay during daytime. Plastic worms can be bought in a toy store or tackle shop for as little as twenty-five cents. I find that the best for fishing are about ten inches long, and purple. All you add is a hook. Plastic worms can imitate the movements of small snakes and eels, and large water salamanders.

PLASTIC WORM

COMMON
WATERSNAKE

SPOTTED
SALAMANDER

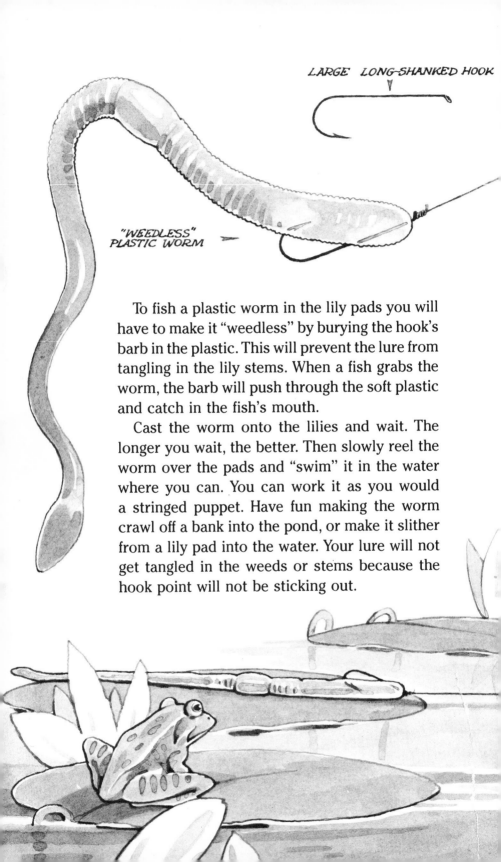

LARGE LONG-SHANKED HOOK

"WEEDLESS"
PLASTIC WORM

To fish a plastic worm in the lily pads you will have to make it "weedless" by burying the hook's barb in the plastic. This will prevent the lure from tangling in the lily stems. When a fish grabs the worm, the barb will push through the soft plastic and catch in the fish's mouth.

Cast the worm onto the lilies and wait. The longer you wait, the better. Then slowly reel the worm over the pads and "swim" it in the water where you can. You can work it as you would a stringed puppet. Have fun making the worm crawl off a bank into the pond, or make it slither from a lily pad into the water. Your lure will not get tangled in the weeds or stems because the hook point will not be sticking out.

Fish, under the lilies, will feel the worm land above them. They will follow it as you pull it over the pads and they will see it drop in the water to swim. Don't be surprised if a monster-sized bass explodes through the lily stems and grabs your lure. If one does, keep your line tight and reel in.

Toward evening sunfish come to the shallows to surface-feed. Bass, bluegills, pumpkinseeds, and crappies may be caught on surface lures. One of the best surface lures is a tiny cork "popping bug." You will need a fly rod and fly line.

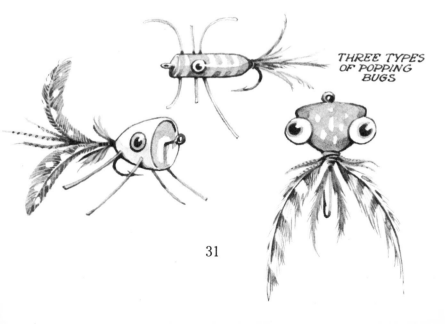

THREE TYPES OF POPPING BUGS

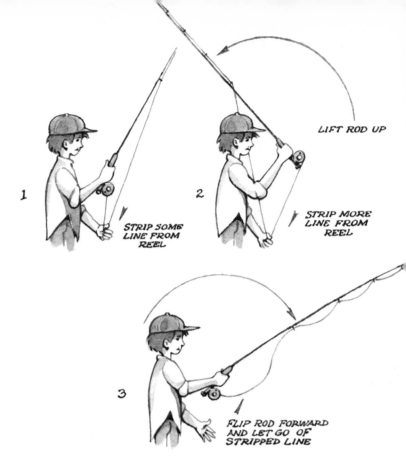

1

2

LIFT ROD UP

STRIP SOME
LINE FROM
REEL

STRIP MORE
LINE FROM
REEL

3

FLIP ROD FORWARD
AND LET GO OF
STRIPPED LINE

Attach the bug to the end of a five-foot nylon leader and cast it by stripping the heavy fly line from your reel and flipping the loose line onto the pond in front of you. The bug will land with a *plop*. This may attract a fish right away because it sounds like a small frog plopping in the water. If not, give the bug a slight twitch by lifting the tip of your rod. This will disturb the surface the way a struggling moth or beetle would. After a few twitches a fat bluegill may snap it under! Once you've reeled in your line, cast and try again.

NATURAL

IMITATION

Casting a fly rod or spinning rod can be clumsy at first. Remember, if your line gets tangled among the brush or weeds, retrieve all the tangled line and bring it home with you. Birds, waterfowl and other wild animals can become hopelessly snarled in strong fishing line.

HOW TO MAKE A CORK POPPING BUG

To make a cork popping bug you will need the smallest cork you can find, a fish hook, two thin rubber bands, a small soft feather, waterproof glue, some enamel paints, and a large sewing needle.

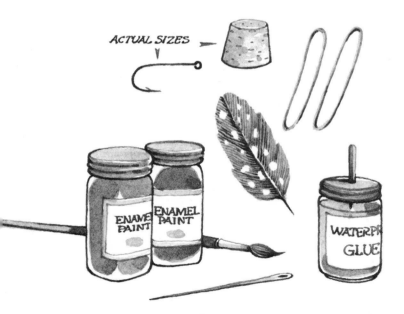

ACTUAL SIZES

With your needle, cut a
slice down the side of the
cork.

Coat the hook's shank with
glue and slide it into the
slice so the point is at the
bottom of the cork and
the eye is at the top. Let
the glue dry.

BE CAREFUL
OF THE SHARP
HOOK POINT

Paint the cork with any
pattern you think a fish
would like (I use yellow
with black strips and
dots). Let it dry.

ERASER USED TO HOLD
CORK WHILE PAINTING

Use the needle to poke
two holes on each side of
the painted cork and one
hole on the bottom of the
cork just above the hook.

ARROWS SHOW
NEEDLE HOLES

SIDES

BACK

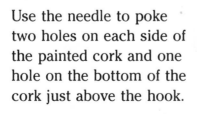

Cut the rubber bands into four one-inch strips and dip each strip's tip in the glue.

USE THESE FOUR STRIPS

CUT HERE

CUT HERE

Now use your needle to push the glues tips of each rubber band strip into each of the holes on the cork's sides.

Dip the feather tip in glue. Insert it in the needle hole at the back of the cork above the hook and you are ready to go

BUGGING FOR BLUEGILLS!

ACTUAL SIZE OF FINISHED BUG

Perch & Pike

A reservoir holds the fresh waters of streams, springs, and rainfall. Its underworld is a valley of plains that once were fields and ledges, once cliffs. Underwater creek currents wind in and out of drowned tree stumps. Above, noisy geese bob on white-capped waves while fishing herons stalk still-water coves. All kinds of fish live here, from perch to pike.

The perch family includes yellow perch and walleyes. Chain pickerel, northern pike, and muskellunge are members of the pike tribe. Many of these, and other fish, thrive in the grab bag of habitats created by a man-made reservoir.

This is big water. Take your time and it will slowly let you in on secrets. If you watch and listen the water will tell you where perch school and pike hunt.

WALLEYE

YELLOW PERCH

MUSKELLUNGE

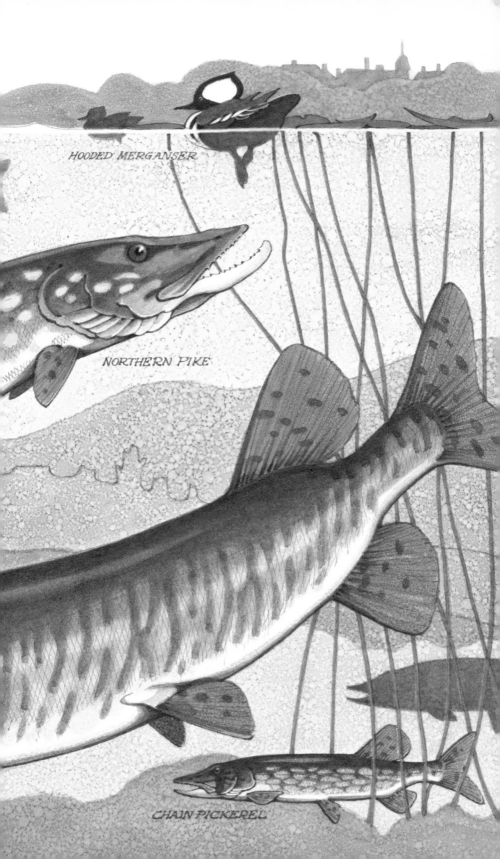

HOODED MERGANSER

NORTHERN PIKE

CHAIN PICKEREL

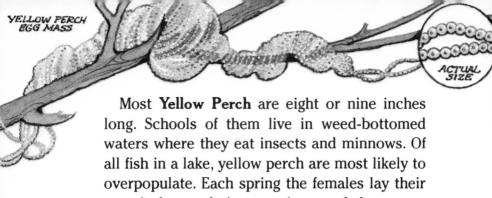

ACTUAL
SIZE

Most **Yellow Perch** are eight or nine inches long. Schools of them live in weed-bottomed waters where they eat insects and minnows. Of all fish in a lake, yellow perch are most likely to overpopulate. Each spring the females lay their eggs in long gelatinous strings, and these eggs are fertilized by the males' milt. One female can lay many thousands of eggs. Newly hatched perch are eaten by fishing birds, snapping turtles, and other fish. This keeps the perch numbers down considerably.

SNAPPING TURTLE

All perch have two separated dorsal fins. These fins are sharply spined. When a yellow perch is seized by an enemy, it spreads these fins wide apart, opening them from back to front. Many fish do this. Because they do, if they are swallowed tail first, the sharp fin spines will lift open and stick in an enemy's throat. This is why predators that swallow their prey whole must swallow fish head first. When a fish is swallowed head first it cannot spread open its fins, so it slides down the eater's throat.

YELLOW PERCH

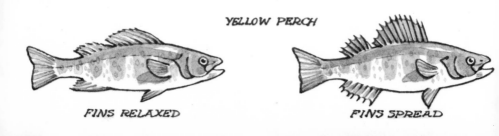

FINS RELAXED   FINS SPREAD

I watched a great blue heron catching one yellow perch after another. Each time the huge bird nabbed a prickly perch from the water with her long beak, she flipped the fish into the air and caught it head first, for swallowing. One perch the heron caught was much larger than the others. It took many comical tries before the bird was able to flip the heavy fish just right. When she did swallow, the fat perch bulged in her skinny neck. Herons look cross-eyed all the time, but I was sure this heron's eyes crossed even further as the wide lump of fish slid down her throat.

Walleyes are the largest perch. These green fish with white bellies can grow to be three feet long. Walleyes are so named because of the white film over their eyeballs. They live in deep waters of lakes or rivers, and eat minnows and crayfish. Walleyes grasp their food in their strong teeth.

In springtime, as soon as snows melt, walleyes swim in masses to the sandy shoals and gravel bars of the lake or river bottom to lay their eggs.

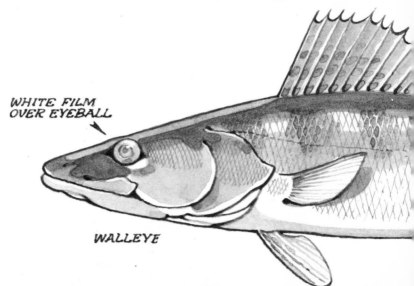

WHITE FILM
OVER EYEBALL

WALLEYE

These hearty fish are very active during rainy, sleet-slashed days when the light is dim, the wind is bitter, and the water is icy cold. You have to be adventurous to be a walleye watcher.

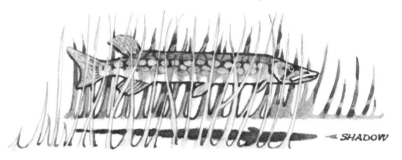

◄ SHADOW

Chain Pickerel blend well with their grassy surroundings. It takes a sharp eye to see these slender predators. I find them in the shallows by looking for their shadows, beneath them. The chain pickerel is a green pike with dark chain-link markings. Typical of the pike family, it has a long flat snout, fully equipped with many needle sharp teeth. Pike are meat eaters. Chain pickerel eat minnows, eels, frogs, and other large fish. When a pickerel catches a fish it manipulates the fish around, to swallow it head first.

Pickerel are the smallest members of the pike family. They average nine to fifteen inches. Chain pickerel like the swampy sections of lakes and streams, where they lurk in very shallow grass beds. When a victim appears, the hunter does not chase, but impatiently waits until the prey gets close enough to be snatched. The pickerel

AMERICAN
EEL

CHAIN PICKEREL

do this so quickly, they can startle you. I am often surprised by the sudden dash of a pickerel in the water. But once I know its hiding spot, I crouch by the water and watch for it to swipe another meal. The best time to watch pickerel is in the spring when all pike spawn in shallow water.

NORTHERN PIKE

The **Northern Pike** is the only pike with light blotches on its sides. "Northerns" grow as large as four feet. Like their smaller pickerel cousins they lie in wait for prey, rather than hunt it down. Northern pike spend the summer in shallows of lakes and rivers. In the winter they seek deeper water.

MUSKRAT

Pike are solitary and always hungry. Even when the surfaces of the lakes have frozen over they will attack anything within striking distance. Northerns eat many fish and frogs, but muskrats and ducks are also pulled under in the toothy clamps of their jaws.

BUFFLEHEAD DUCK

Look for these large fish in weed beds where their blotched sides blend with the water's dappled light.

43

MINK FROG

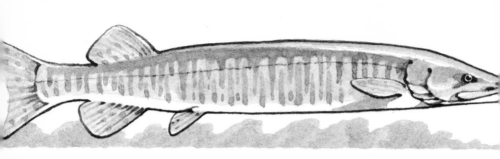

The **Muskellunge** is the king of freshwater fish and the largest of the pikes. They are giants, some growing to five feet and longer, but many "muskies" are the same size as northern pike. Look for the dark blotches on a muskellunge's side to tell it from its pike relatives.

Muskies spawn in springtime shallows, just before they retreat to deep water for the summer. In the fall they return to the shallow water, to spend the winter. During this time they go on a feeding spree, and it is possible to find them thrashing after anything that moves in the weed beds. They do not wait for food to come to them. They hunt it down. But if a musky sees you, it will bolt away.

Muskellunge are found in more places than their northern pike cousins. Many reservoirs and recreation lakes near large cities have muskies living in them.

They are elusive fish, but bold. Often a giant musky will appear suddenly and make a pass at some object in the water. A flashing lunch spoon accidentally dropped from a boat, or a crimson maple leaf falling on the lake can trigger a musky to strike. When this happens, these alligator-sized fish can make your heart thump wildly.

WHAT HAPPENS TO FISH IN THE WINTER?

I know a tiny pond where goldfish live each winter encased in solid ice. This also happens to many fish in the wild. When perch get trapped in a completely frozen pool, they can live as long as their barely pulsing bodies do not also freeze solid. When the water thaws they become active again.

Fish are extremely sensitive to temperature changes. When the water around them becomes too cold or too warm, they must find water that's more comfortable. Some migrate to deep water in the winter. Others winter in the shallows. There are fish that alter their life style in the winter. Brook trout are not school fish, but in winter they congregate in deep stream pools while their autumn-spawned eggs develop in upstream gravel.

There are fish that feed all winter. People catch crappies, perch, pike, and trout through holes in the ice. Some fish, like smallmouth bass, become lazy in the winter. They barely move or feed. Catfish nestle into the mud for the cold months. Rock bass are hibernators. Of course, fish that live in warm climates carry on business as usual during the winter.

CATFISH NESTLED
IN MUD

The wobbling motion of a spoon in the water attracts fish. Bass, bluegills, crappies, perch, and pike will strike the flashing metal of "spoon" lures. Small spoon lures cost about twenty-five cents. Larger ones cost more.

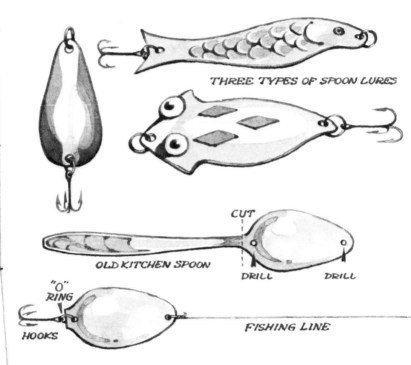

THREE TYPES OF SPOON LURES

OLD KITCHEN SPOON

CUT

DRILL   DRILL

"O" RING

HOOKS

FISHING LINE

You can make a large spoon lure out of an old kitchen spoon, an "O-ring," and a set of triple hooks. Saw the handle off and have someone drill two holes in the spoon, one at the tip for your line and one at the bottom for the O-ring that will hold the hooks.

CASTING ROD
AND REEL

46

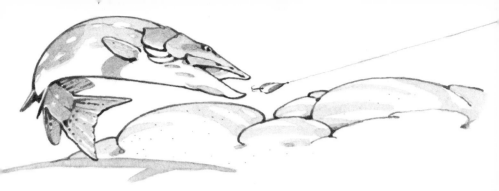

Tie your lure to your line with a strong knot and cast. Spoons wobble in the water and flash in the light all by themselves. All you have to do is reel them in. You can cast to deep water and retrieve it or along the shallow shore and reel it back. There is no mistaking when you hook a fish on a spoon. Fish strike them quick and hard.

Use tiny metal spoons for small fish and big silver spoons for big fish. For northern pike and muskies you will need a short wire leader that won't snap in their sharp teeth. Most metal lures have triple hooks. Be careful when you handle them, and when you catch a fish, remove each hook point slowly. You can make hooks easier to unhook by bending each hook's barb down with a narrow pliers. This will help prevent damaging tears in the fish's mouth or in your fingers. Small pike are too bony to eat. A fish caught on a wobbling spoon can be released safely.

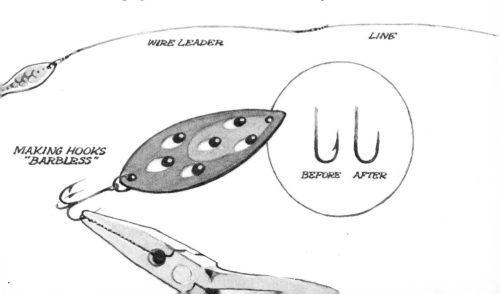

WIRE LEADER

LINE

MAKING HOOKS "BARBLESS"

BEFORE   AFTER

When you catch a sharp-toothed pike, hold the fish firmly behind the gills with one hand and carefully remove the hooks with the other. Watch out for those teeth!

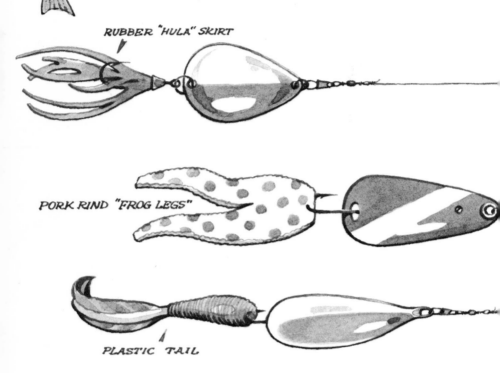

RUBBER "HULA" SKIRT

PORK RIND "FROG LEGS"

PLASTIC TAIL

You can buy rubber skirts, plastic tails, and pork rinds that can be added to the hooks of a spoon. These wave in the water, coaxing fish to bite. They also help make the wobbling lure weedless for fishing in the lily pads or weedy waters.

To make a tail for your spoon lure you will need a small, round, rubber balloon and a pair of scissors.

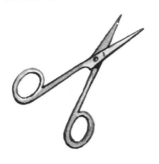

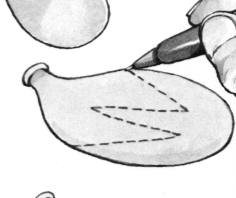

Lay the balloon flat and draw a tail pattern on it with a ball-point pen.

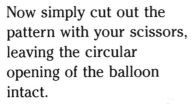

Now simply cut out the pattern with your scissors, leaving the circular opening of the balloon intact.

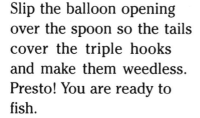

Slip the balloon opening over the spoon so the tails cover the triple hooks and make them weedless. Presto! You are ready to fish.

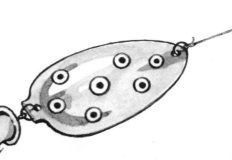

Catfish & Carp

he creek's mud-brown water flows slowly. There is no hurry. Sultry air is alive with the buzzing of insects and singing of birds. Plant-choked backwaters edge a nearby field where a marsh hawk picks a vole from the grasses. Mud turtles rest on a sun-scorched dock. And summer cottages line a shore that once knew only the Indian's tread. This is catfish country.

Catfish and carp are at home in warm, weedy, mud-bottomed water. Both are bottom feeders and are more active at night than they are during the day. You'll find them in secluded lakes and neighborhood creeks.

With catfish and carp we complete our fresh-water journey from the spirited tumble of mountain streams to the easy flow of coastal creeks.

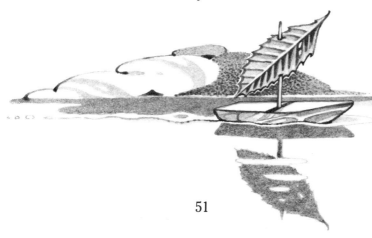

FEELER

BARB

The **Bullhead Catfish** is the most common member of the catfish family. Catfish are named for long feelers on their faces that look like cat whiskers. Bullheads are brown above and yellow below. They can grow to be twenty inches long.

All catfish have sharp barbs on their pectoral fins that inject poison when they jab an enemy. To people, catfish "stings" are no worse than insect bites. Remember, it is their fin barbs that sting, not their whiskers.

Bullhead catfish will eat anything from snails to aquatic plants. They rarely come near the surface and, because of their muddy coloring, are hard to detect in the water. But in the spring thousands of spawning bullheads can be seen crowding the shallow water of lake-feeding streams. Here the females lay their eggs in a sand nest. The males fertilize the eggs. Both male and female guard the eggs and also the hatched fry. Then the father takes charge and teaches the baby bullheads how to find food and avoid danger.

FATHER
CATFISH
AND FRY

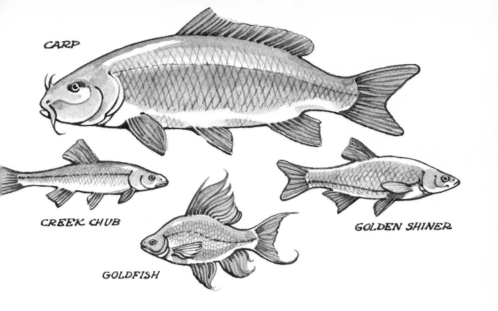

CARP

CREEK CHUB

GOLDFISH

GOLDEN SHINER

The common **Carp** is an Asian native that was brought to America in the last century. Carp are members of one of the largest fish families, the minnows. Although carp can grow to be thirty pounds or bigger, most minnows are small, averaging from two to ten inches. They are important as food for predatory fish, birds, and animals. Creek chubs, shiners, dace, and even fancy goldfish are all smaller minnow relatives of carp.

Carp are orange fish, heavily scaled. They have feelers on their face, as catfish do, and like catfish, they eat plant life, insects, and crayfish.

Carp are wary fish. However, early in summer, when they are spawning, it is possible to stalk them closely. Spawning carp are easy to find in a lake or stream. They are noisy. Listen for their loud splashes and clumsy flops in the shallow water.

RED-WINGED
BLACKBIRD
(FEMALE)

DAMSELFLY

BULL FROG

BULLFROG
TADPOLE

RED~WINGED
BLACKBIRD
(MALE)

CARP

BROWN BULLHEAD
CATFISH

DAMSELFLY
NYMPH

FISHING FOR CATFISH & CARP

Carp and catfish find their food by smell. It is not necessary to attract them with movement or sound. "Still fishing" a smelly doughball will catch both of these bottom feeders. You will need a casting or spinning rod, a few split-shot sinkers, and a medium-sized hook.

SPLIT~SHOT

Making doughballs for fishing is easy. Pour one-half cup of flour, one-half cup of cornmeal, three tablespoons of water, and one tablespoon of cod-liver oil into a mixing bowl. Knead it with your hands to a workable dough, and that's it! The dough can be wrapped in foil and stored in the refrigerator.

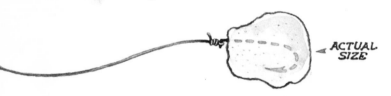

ACTUAL SIZE

When you go fishing take a small wad of dough and ball it around your hook. Pinch two split-shot sinkers on your line, about twelve inches above the doughball, cast it as far as you can out into the water, and wait.

YELLOWTHROAT WARBLER

Still fishing takes patience. Bring your binoculars along. You'll be surprised how far you can travel between bites. Explore the shore on the other side of the lake, or glimpse small birds in nearby bushes. Once I followed a skein of honking geese over the horizon and got back just in time to reel in a whopper. Don't be discouraged if you don't feel a nibble right away. When you do get a tug, wait until the line goes taut and reel in. You may have a battle on your hands, hauling a huge thrashing carp to shore!

If you catch a catfish, hold it firmly with one hand, keeping its side fins and sharp barbs pressed flat. Then work the hook out with your free hand. Don't let their homely looks keep you from eating catfish. They are meaty fish and delicious fried in flour and cornmeal.

The best time to fish for catfish and carp is at night, when each tug on your line is a message from another world.

Cleaning your Catch

Here is an easy way to prepare your fish for the frying pan. If you do it carefully, there is no scaling and very little mess. You will need a sharp knife and a pair of pliers. Always be careful when using a knife. Never face the blade toward you. Ask Mom or Dad to help.

Cut the dorsal fins off with one long slice.

Cut a line in the skin behind the gills on each side of your fish. Leave the head on.

Grasp the fish's skin with your pliers and, holding the head firmly, pull the scales and skin off. Do the other side the same way.

Remove the head, breast bones, and insides with one cut as shown.

Now cut off the tail and your fish is ready for the pan.

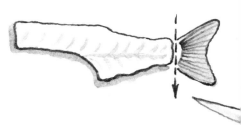

All fish but trout can be cleaned this way. Trout have little or no scales. So when you clean a trout, all you have to do is remove the fish's insides and wash the meat under water. Trout are eaten with their skin on. In fact, the skin is very tasty.

Always eat fish slowly to enjoy the fresh-caught flavor and to be on the alert for sharp bones in the meat. And remember, the parts of your catch that you don't eat can be buried in the garden to fertilize the soil. If you live in the city and don't have a garden, clean your fish at the lake and put the leftovers neatly under a bush for the raccoons to find and eat.

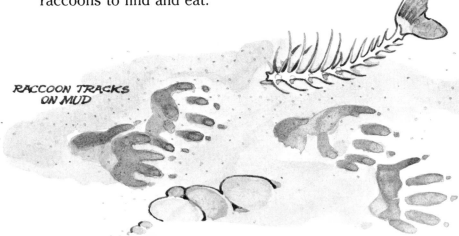

RACCOON TRACKS
ON MUD

Pumpkinseed   *Hall's Lake – April 1981*
caught by Amber Arnosky

Making a Fish Print

Those special fish you will want to remember even after they are eaten can be printed and saved. Before you prepare the fish for cooking brush one of its sides with edible food coloring. Place a piece of paper carefully on the coated fish and press gently with your hands. Mold the paper around the fish so its dorsal fins and bottom fins print. Remove the paper carefully.

It may take a few tries to get a good print. You may have to add more food coloring and try again. When you do make a nice print, you can work over the rough areas with a pencil or even color the print in the fish's natural hues.

Lastly, cut out your finished print and paste it flat on a stiff board.

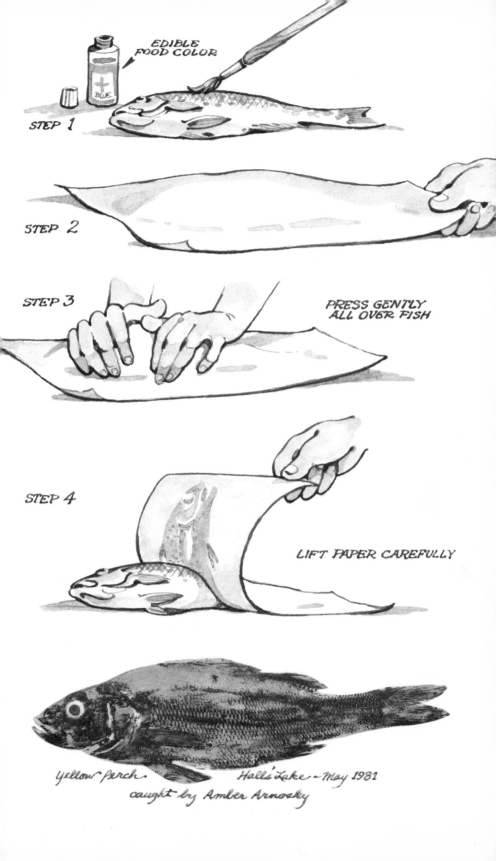

EDIBLE FOOD COLOR

BLUE

STEP 1

STEP 2

STEP 3

PRESS GENTLY ALL OVER FISH

STEP 4

LIFT PAPER CAREFULLY

Yellow Perch. Hall's Lake ~ May 1981
caught by Amber Arnosky

Fishing Knots

∽ CLINCH KNOT ∽

*THIS IS THE BEST KNOT TO USE WHEN
ATTACHING LINE TO A HOOK OR LURE.*

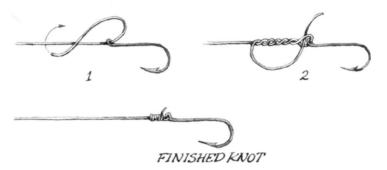

FINISHED KNOT

∽ BLOOD KNOT ∽

*USE THIS KNOT WHEN YOU ARE JOINING
TWO LINES OF THE SAME THICKNESS.*

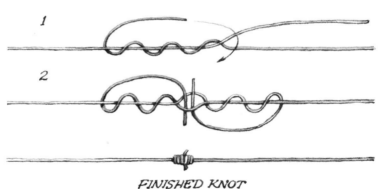

FINISHED KNOT

62

~ TYING AN EYE LOOP ~

THIS KNOT IS USED TO PREPARE A LENGTH
OF LEADER TO ATTACH IT TO A HEAVY FLY LINE.

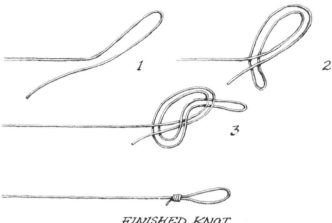

1

2

3

FINISHED KNOT

~ LEADER TO FLY LINE ~

THIS KNOT WILL ATTACH A NYLON LEADER
TO THE END OF HEAVY FLY LINE.

1 TIE A KNOT
IN THE VERY TIP
OF HEAVY FLY LINE.

2

3

FINISHED KNOT

ABOUT THE AUTHOR

Jim Arnosky has illustrated many articles for *Fly Fisherman* and *Rod & Reel.* He is also the author and illustrator of over twenty-five books for young readers, including *Outdoors on Foot, Kettle of Hawks, I Was Born in a Tree and Raised by Bees,* and the popular sequel, *Crinkleroot's Animal Tracks and Wildlife Signs,* as well as *Raindrop Stories,* which was published by Four Winds Press. Mr. Arnosky lives with his wife and daughters on a farm called "Ramtails" overlooking the Wells River in South Ryegate, Vermont.